Introduction

I began teaching p
something I had antic
wanted to make the
wonderful job.

CH00923065

Personal financial
education' and most
active participants in
unchallenged many of society's assumptions and values.

The consumer society pressurises us to submit and fit in – to allow our individuality to be shaped by market forces. Almost everything has a price tag and the marketing is inescapable. But when people spend their money like everyone else, they severely limit their ability to be true to themselves and what they believe. This is especially true of Christians. I think the reason Christ taught so much about money and wealth in the Sermon on the Mount was so we would not be hindered from living the way he described by the financial risks it involves.

So that there is no misunderstanding, I should be clear that this book is **not** a guide to personal finance. It includes an explanation of why personal financial education is important but it is mainly an attempt to explain money and an appeal to develop a healthy relationship with it.

If you are worried about your financial situation, or if you need help with debt, you should get expert help. Free local advice centres are listed in telephone directories and at public libraries; for immediate help, call National Debtline on 0808 808 4000 or go to the website www.nationaldebtline.co.uk.

I circulated an early version of this book among the staff and volunteers at All Souls Clubhouse in October 2011. As I am sure the text will continue to evolve, if you see some things differently, please do get in touch with me.

Philip Evans
e-mail: philipevans@clubhousew1.org

Origins & Evolution

Money was invented in different parts of the world at different times but the first time may have been somewhere in China, around BC 1200. When we read in Genesis that Jacob's sons took bundles of money to Egypt to buy corn, the 'money' was probably silver rings of equal weight tied together in bundles of equal weight.

Banking and credit existed long before money and are thought to have originated in ancient Babylon, where palaces and temples were the safest places to store precious metals, grain and fabrics. Even there, however, they were vulnerable, which is why Christ referred to earthly treasures that moths and rust destroy or thieves break in and steal.

The earliest form of credit was probably the loan of seed to be repaid by a share of the harvest: these loans were made in the name of the ruler or deity associated with the 'bank'. This is what Joseph did in Egypt, towards the end of the seven years of famine, when he gave seed in Pharaoh's name in exchange for a fifth of the harvest.

The first coins were made at Lydia in Asia Minor in around BC 678: the word 'money' derives from the name of the local goddess, Moneta. The Jews first used coins on their return to Israel after the exile in Babylon: they may have been reluctant to use them because they would have stamped on them the images of foreign rulers and pagan gods. Israel started to make its own coins in about BC 140 and the first moneychangers at the Temple may have performed a much appreciated service for visiting Jews by exchanging their foreign coins for ones they were happier to use.

Money was invented to make it easier for people to exchange goods and services; without it, communities could not have grown and the public services we take for granted today would not be possible. But money has evolved beyond a tool, even an indispensable one. Economic theory is now regarded as a primary means of studying and explaining human life; the creation of wealth through capitalism is seen as the way to satisfy people; money is the global status symbol that promises freedom, security, purpose, power, happiness – and even love. Some people make the accumulation of money their life's goal; others see it as the path to fulfilment or the things it can buy as defining who they are. It takes more than a few paragraphs to sum up the consumer society we live in but the following set the scene.

- Money is so important in almost every area of life that it is very difficult to express the value of anything except as price or cost.

- Goods and services are available 24/7 so that, assuming you can pay the price, you can have what you want 'out of season' or from anywhere in the world.

- 'Instant' credit means that you do not necessarily have to be able to afford what you want to buy and can act on a whim.

- Psychology has empowered marketing, advertising and sales talk to exploit basic human needs like security, self-esteem and significance. This manipulates us into buying what we neither need nor previously wanted.

- As acquisition has become so important to personal self-esteem and social worth, 'honesty' has become increasingly subjective.

Some forms of deceit have become so commonplace that we no longer think of them as dishonest but simply the way things are done today. Supermarkets promote 'special offers' that, in fact, are more expensive than usual. Sales people cold-call us, claiming to be conducting or following up surveys; others claim they know about our credit deals, PPI (Payment Protection Insurance) or mobile phone contracts. Representatives from utility companies visit our homes claiming to be investigating the misuse of tariffs but really want us to switch to them. Building companies send people to conduct property inspections but they are really touting for work. Many salespeople introduce themselves using carefully chosen words designed to create the impression they have some official status or are acting on behalf of a public authority, like a local council.

The breakdown of a shared morality has led to high levels of personal dishonesty and mutual mistrust. Putting false information on credit applications and inventing or inflating insurance claims is widespread. High majorities of people admit to pilfering from employers, restaurants and hotels. Our 'default position' when looking for tradesmen and other service providers is to expect to be cheated with poor service or over-charging. Whenever we make a complaint about faulty goods or deficient work, we can expect to be treated with suspicion, as if we are making it up.

Money: Tool or Tyrant?

People have always failed to control money adequately. In *A History of Money*, Professor Glyn Davies observes that, 'Despite man's growing mastery of science and technology, he has so far been unable to master money, at any rate with any acceptable degree of success, and to the extent that it has succeeded, the irrecoverable costs in terms of mass unemployment and lost output would seem to outweigh the benefits.' Why is this?

Although money has great symbolism and objective power, it is not real: it is a system of trust based upon shared assumptions about the value of things. Money has physical presence in the real world but it is the same sort of reality as a novel: it is 'real' only in that it gives expression to an idea. This is why we cannot control money with precision or certainty: the best we can do is to try to control the factors that control money.

Individuals have significant control over their income and spending, yet nobody behaves entirely rationally and from time to time we all make mistakes and do daft things that have financial consequences. We are also hindered by events beyond our control, like the availability of work or when things break down and have to be repaired or replaced.

It is harder for families to control money, because of the diverse behaviour patterns of the individual members; it is very much harder for companies and nations. The Eurozone is in continuing crisis because the range of conflicting factors are beyond the control of any one person or government.

Although we try to make fiction real in many ways, it is never really real and the extent to which it affects our lives depends on how we relate to it. We make novels seem more real by turning them into television programmes and films, so we can watch people act out the stories. Or we produce reference books that describe the fiction as if it were real, like biographies of Sherlock Holmes and tour guides for Tolkien's Middle-Earth. We can get more involved when the fiction becomes a computer game, where we are part of the story and our own abilities and preferences affect the plot. Today, people create wholly fictional lives for themselves by means of avatars living in virtual worlds imagined in cyberspace.

When people are obsessed with fiction, they can become unbalanced in real life: they cease to make clear distinctions about what is important or understand what is acceptable behaviour. In the same way, obsession with money often changes people for the worse, distorting their perceptions and priorities.

Medical research has shown that making money can produce the same sort of 'high' as cocaine, by stimulating the same area of the brain. This goes some way to explaining the escalating selfishness, greed and recklessness that drives people to sacrifice their relationships, neglect their families and ruin their health for money!

This danger of intoxication is why 'wealth gurus' usually advise people to define the lifestyle they want and then calculate how rich they need to be to live it, rather than to risk ruining their lives chasing abstract wealth. But Christ had something even more malevolent in mind when he said that we cannot serve both God and mammon.

Some Bibles translate the word mammon in Matthew 6:24 and Luke 16:9 as 'money' but there is a difference. Mammon is money personified; money that influences behaviour. This might sound as if money is a personality with a will, and in the past some Christians have thought of mammon as a demon, but it is an impersonal force, like the force of an idea whose time has come. The ways that people relate to money gives it power over them and when enough people behave that way the whole of society begins to revolve around money.

When Christ referred to mammon, he was using a concept from ancient Babylon. Historians used to look back to the Romans or Greeks for the seeds of modern civilisation but increasingly they now look further back, to Babylon. There were no idols called mammon in Babylon, and no temples dedicated to it, but life there revolved around money as if it were the State religion.

This way of thinking continued down through the centuries. Many historians believe that major world events were the product of financial catastrophes and innovations; others go further and believe that they were the consequence of financial pressures and greed manipulating people's self-interest. This is mammon, operating in the background, many steps removed from the action, like a pagan idol; it is why today we expect to be able to pay for things that previous generations could only pray for.

Real Dangers

Our relationship with money is as crucial to our well-being as our skill at handling it. Psychologists have found that people with 'loose' attitudes towards money tend to be happier than those who are more controlling. Nevertheless, they are no less likely to be materialists, and no less prone to overspending and debt, and therefore just as vulnerable to the same mental and emotional problems.

Professor E Thomas Garman's research in America, and research published in 2004 by Royal Holloway University in London, demonstrate that people with money problems are less able to work and study because the mental and emotional burden blunts their creativity, intuitiveness and productivity. The Royal Holloway research found that students with money problems did less well in their final exams than anticipated.

This is all on top of the more fundamental and widespread problems caused by materialism. Dr Oliver James, author of *Affluenza* and *The Selfish Capitalist*, describes how people with an undue emphasis on money, possessions, entertainments, appearances and status are particularly vulnerable to emotional disorders. This can plunge them into a downward spiral, as they seek to relieve their feelings of insecurity, inadequacy and depression by buying what they think will bring relief and happiness.

Historically, the church has considered both avarice (the love of money) and covetousness (the desire for possessions, experiences and status) to be 'deadly' sins. They were deadly because they could kill your soul, the real you, and your relationship with God. The demons of avarice and covetousness were portrayed in the front line of the devil's army because they wounded believers, leaving them vulnerable to other sins, such as vanity, pride, jealousy, greed, gluttony, deceit, anger, selfishness and strife.

While I do not think there is a necessary distinction to be made between deadly and venal (or excusable) sins, or am convinced there are demons called avarice and covetousness, the dangers of materialism and wealth were seen much more clearly in the past. In the 4th Century, John Chrysostom wrote:

For a dreadful, a dreadful thing is the love of money, it disables both eyes and ears, and makes men worse to deal with than a wild beast, allowing a man to consider neither conscience, nor friendship, nor fellowship, nor the salvation of his own soul, but having withdrawn them at once from all these things, like some harsh mistress, it makes those captured by it its slaves. And the dreadful part of so bitter a slavery is, that it persuades them even to be grateful for it...

The Root of Infidelity

'The love of money is the root of all evil.' So many generations of Christians have grown up in a consumer society that we have come to see these words of the Apostle Paul in 1 Timothy 6 as a general observation that, like all generalisations, is not entirely accurate. Many modern translations, like the English Standard Version that I usually quote, therefore say that the love of money is 'a root of *all kinds of evil*'. This is an accurate translation but, in view of everything else in the Bible about money and wealth, I think the traditional translation conveys the truth more accurately.

The phrase 'all kinds of' is never used in a literal sense because the word 'all' is not inclusive: it does not mean 'every', as it usually does, but 'many'. If we say that a shop sells all kinds of sweets, we do not mean that it sells every variety of sweets made, only that it sells lots of different kinds. But when Paul wrote to Timothy he was not warning that people who desire to be rich risk getting into all sorts of trouble and distress, and leaving open the possibility there are other roots of evil. He was warning that they have the same ambition that lies at the very origin of evil.

In Isaiah 14, from verse 12 onwards, we read words originally attributed to Nebuchadnezzar, King of Babylon, but which many think are applicable to Lucifer, the angel that rebelled against God and became the devil. In Genesis 3, we read how the devil enticed Eve into eating the forbidden fruit. Crucially, neither Lucifer nor Eve wanted to be God: what they both wanted was to be *like* God.[1] This ambition included autonomy and self-aggrandisement.

---

[1] Compare Isaiah 14:14 with Genesis 3:5.

Similar self-reliance, pride and vanity were behind building the Tower of Babel; they were behind Nebuchadnezzar's grand projects to develop Babylon and his desire to conquer the holy city of Jerusalem. It was this sort of self-sufficiency and self-fulfilment the devil sought to provoke when he tempted Christ in the wilderness. In James' epistle, the boasting of the business people who made their plans for prosperity without reference to God is branded not just arrogant but 'evil'!

In the past, Christians often dealt with avarice and covetousness as the same sin but, as money has evolved into a system of pure trust, the truth that Paul saw has become easier for us to see. Coin collectors may covet particular coins for their value or rarity or beauty but avarice drives people to accumulate money for its power. Money is what people use to meet their needs and fulfil their ambitions; it is what they use to get things and to get things done; it is how they make their way in society and their mark on history. It is what they devote themselves to when they will not serve God.

By describing the love of money as a root, Paul illustrates how it ruins lives. A root is an ugly tangle that grows underground, out of sight, from where it feeds flowers and fruit that look and taste very different. It follows that if you want to know if you have avarice, do not dig around in the darkness of your unconscious mind for the root but look for the fruit and flowers in your life: sins like the greed, vanity, excess, pretention, ostentation, snobbery, selfishness and so many others that the celebrity culture admires as virtues.

Personal Financial Education

Personal financial education is widely misunderstood and so it is probably easiest to begin by explaining what it is not.

- It is not debt advice or counselling. Debt advisers do at least four things: help the person in debt to maximise their income, show them where they could save money, verify exactly how much they owe and negotiate on their behalf with their creditors.

- It is not money guidance. This is where money advisers help people choose suitable financial products. They may, for example, identify a selection of bank accounts, utility tariffs or insurance options and then talk through how to choose the most suitable ones.

- It is not financial or investment advice. Although personal financial education can explain how investments and pensions work, and how to choose sensibly, it will not recommend specific products or help people to obtain them.

Personal financial education equips and empowers people to make their own good choices and to understand the limits of their own competence. Just as when trying to fix a computer problem or a car engine, it is good to know when to give up and seek expert help to avoid making a bad situation worse. Furthermore, education equips people to make the best use of this help. Although a salesperson may explain savings plans, insurance policies or mobile phone tariffs fairly, customers need to be able to evaluate that information. Many debt repayment plans negotiated by debt advisers fail within about six weeks because the people in debt did not properly understand their predicament or give their advisers enough good information about their overall financial situation.

Effective financial education motivates changes in behaviour, such as creating a budget, reducing credit card and overdraft balances, saving, planning for retirement and starting an emergency fund that reduces dependence on credit and insurance. It should result in people having fewer liabilities and increased net worth. Research indicates that people who act on financial education are, after about 10 years, on average better off by a whole year's income.

More important than the financial benefits, people who handle their money well can live better quality lives. We daily face an army of advertisers and sales people trying to circumvent our rationale and target our emotions, so that we will buy new clothes, cosmetics, fashion accessories, gadgets, entertainments and holidays. But if we spend our money in ways that suit other people, we cannot use it to meet our own priorities or to develop our own unique character and abilities.

Personal financial education can therefore do a great deal of good helping people to identify personal preferences and exercise personal freedom. It can help them challenge consumerism and materialism and live with greater contentment, whether they have plenty or little.

Removing Obstacles to Faith & Maturity

Financial education is not evangelism but it can be evangelistic by clearing a path for the Gospel. Christ said that it is harder for a rich person to enter the Kingdom of God than for a camel to crawl through the eye of a needle. He said it after an encounter with a devout, rich young ruler who could not bring himself to transfer the trust he had in his inherited wealth to God alone by experiencing voluntary poverty.[2]

By comparison with our grandparents and with most of the people living in the world today, we in the UK are rich! This affluence occupies us with secondary things: not having to worry about where our next meal is coming from, we worry about how it will taste; having many clothes to choose from, we fret about our image; with too much leisure time, we strive for novelty. Affluence can build addiction to routine comfort that undermines inner values and higher priorities and corrupt the very qualities we need to enter the Kingdom of God, like teachability, trust and child-like dependence.

In *Money and the Meaning of Life*, Professor Jacob Needleman, writes, 'Theoretically, philosophically, I may be quite willing to accept that there is a higher reality... But when it comes to money – ah, that is usually quite a different matter... Everywhere [money] is still understood, often even more forcibly than in matters of illness and death, as

---

[2] See Matthew 19:16-30, Mark 10:17-31 & Luke 18:18-30.

representing the "real world" – the "bottom line".' I think that describes the situation of many people: whatever they believe about 'God', they are persistently distracted by the immediate demands of money and materialism.

These problems often remain after people commit themselves to Christ, as old ways of thinking and acting can be difficult to shake off. In the parables of the sower, Christ likened the cares of this world, the deceitfulness of riches, the desires for things and the pleasures of life to thorns that choke the Word of God and Christian growth, so that no 'fruit' is bought to 'maturity'. Paul was explicit that Christians 'who desire to be rich fall into temptation and a snare, and into many foolish and harmful lusts which drown men in destruction and perdition'. Among the sins that prevent Christians receiving their inheritance in the Kingdom of God are covetousness, theft, extortion, selfish ambition, jealousy, contentions and sorcery.[3]

Like personal financial education generally, we should first eliminate some misconceptions about what constitutes a distinctly 'Christian' approach to money.

- It is not seeking a middle way between a traditional Christian austerity, like the vow of poverty expected of 'spiritual' people, and the extravagance of modern materialism and consumerism.

- It is not giving-led. Many Christians are driven by the fear that God will not bless them, and may punish them, if they do not give.

Malachi 3 speaks about the consequences of 'robbing God' and this frightens some Christians into thinking that God will not bless them if they do not give. Some believe in mandatory

---

[3] See Matthew 13:1-23, Mark 4:1-9 & Luke 8:4-8; I Timothy 6:1-19; I Corinthians 6:9-10, Galatians 5:19-21 & Ephesians 5:1-5. See also Matthew 15:10-20 & Mark 7:14-23. Sorcery (or witchcraft), which is in Paul's list of the 'works of the flesh' in Galatians 5, is not primarily occultic but the human ability to manipulate people's thinking and behaviour.

tithing, which is usually understood to be giving 10% of our income to church, while others see a more general principle of 'sowing and reaping', such as explained in 2 Corinthians 9, as establishing a direct link between giving and blessing. A failure to tithe or to 'sow', they believe, invokes God's displeasure.

Neither tithing nor sowing and reaping imply some sort of automated payback for generosity. Of course, God is pleased with obedience but the deeper purpose of obedience is to transform us into people who can be trusted with blessing. If, however, our giving is motivated by what we hope to receive back, we are testing a spiritual principle, and testing God, rather than doing what is right in simple obedience.

What, then, is the 'Christian' way with money? Sometime after meeting the rich young ruler, Jesus met a tax collector named Zacchaeus, who was prepared to change his allegiance from money to trust God unequivocally.[4] Although he had profited from the dubious practices of his profession, he undertook to give half of his possessions to the poor and to repay everyone he had cheated four times over. Zacchaeus was an accountant and knew this meant not only the end of his fortune but also, if he began to do his job honestly, the end of his comfortable lifestyle. He realised that money would not be nearly so important to him from then onwards.

Christ's Paradigm

The Sermon on the Mount has been called Christ's manifesto of the Kingdom of God. In it, he explains how his followers are to live and includes, in the passage from Matthew 6 that appears on the back cover of this book, his paradigm for handling money. There are three principles.

- Do not worry or fret about material things like food and clothing – or anything else that money can buy.[5]

---

[4] Luke 19:2-10.
[5] Some translations of Matthew 6:25 say 'take no thought' or 'do not be careful' but they go too far. Worry and anxiety are what Christ prohibits, not sensible thought and responsible planning.

- Make seeking God's Kingdom and righteousness the sole lifestyle priority, living as Christ described elsewhere in the Sermon.

- Trust God for basic needs.

Paul wrote something very similar in 1 Timothy 6:6-12, when he warned about the dangers of loving money:

- Be content with food and clothing.

- Flee avarice and greed.

- Pursue righteousness, godliness, faith, love, steadfastness and gentleness.

The Kingdom of God does not function like Western society. In the Kingdom, the first shall be last, the poor and those who suffer are blessed, the meek inherit the earth and the humble are exalted. The leaders are those who serve. It is where we 'turn the other cheek' to those who abuse us and do good to our enemies. The devotional and charitable actions done in secret are openly rewarded by God but the ones done 'to be seen' by people are (at best) of temporal advantage only. The money given to the poor buys incorruptible treasure in heaven but the treasures hoarded on earth are lost to theft and decay. Victory comes out of perceived defeat: this is the way of the cross!

It follows that Christians should not use money like everyone else. It is not just unnecessary but contrary to how things are done in the Kingdom of God. Although the Bible speaks of greater dangers in prosperity than austerity, there is no sin in having money; there is no sin in inheriting wealth or pursuing a career that may bring wealth. The sin is in *wanting to be rich* because this will inevitably drive us to make choices inconsistent with the sort of lifestyle Christ described.

The impact of this can be seen when we start to think about living the lifestyle that Christ described in the Sermon. In the passage on plain speaking (chapter 5:33-37), he advocated honesty in every situation because a system of socially acceptable deceit had built up around the Torah. If someone 'swore by the altar', it was not to be taken so seriously as if they swore by the gift they had sacrificed on the altar.[6] Today, we might hear someone saying, 'Let me be frank...' or 'I'm going to level with you...', suggesting, albeit implicitly, that they might not always be so truthful! Although oral agreements are as legally binding as written contracts, people often say things they do not mean knowing that we will not be able to prove it later, as happens in sales talk and on telephone helplines.

In the passage on exceeding unreasonable demands made by people (5:38-42), the 'wickedness' was not illegality but taking advantage of people *within* the law, often from a position of political or social superiority.

The slap on the cheek was a formal challenge, not the start of a brawl. It was like tossing down a gauntlet in later generations or a solicitor's letter today. Rich people and big business may threaten legal action to quash justified criticism or simply to force their will on people, knowing that others cannot afford to defend the case in court.

Being taken to court for our tunic represents harsh action by creditors. Today this can happen because debt collection systems and court procedures are highly automated. For example, local authority officials who are quick to take people to court for non-payment of council tax, indifferent to how the expensive extra costs will exacerbate poor people's financial problems. Or magistrates who punish poverty-related crime with heavy fines and court officials who add significantly to the hardship by routinely instructing bailiffs to enforce them.[7]

---

[6] See Matthew 23:16-22.

[7] I am not trying to make a political point here but only giving commonplace examples of how financial considerations trump in most areas of life, even in a modern democracy with a developed charter of human rights and a reputation for justice. If public servants are tasked to meet performance targets, ones usually founded on financial imperatives, in order to keep their jobs and advance their careers, they will not often think too deeply about the implications of what they are doing.

Going the extra mile illustrates inconvenient and sometimes unfair demands made by State officials: a Roman solider in an occupied country could require a citizen to carry his baggage and equipment for one mile. Today, we might be stopped by police officers or ticketed by parking attendants for minor, technical infringements with mitigating circumstances because they have their own performance targets to meet. Or we might have to put up with doctor's surgeries that will not give appointments because they would fall outside the NHS target for waiting times. Or bus drivers who do not stop for passengers because they are catching up with their schedule in order to avoid their own financial penalties.

By telling us to love our enemies and those who persecute us (5:44-48), Christ created an obligation towards our colleagues who we compete with for pay rises and promotions and our business rivals with whom we battle for market share. Their tactics can be unscrupulous: manipulating statistics, misrepresenting resources, starting rumours, sabotaging computers – and the rest. Although the ways we love our enemies will not be the same as how we love our friends, the obligation stands. We will not expect our friends to lie to us or about us, for example, and so some caution is necessary when dealing with competitors and adversaries, but when a need is clear and genuine we ought to respond to it kindly. Paul seems to recognise this and expands the point in Romans 12:19-21.

Never avenge yourselves, but leave it to the wrath of God, for it is written, 'Vengeance is mine, I will repay, says the Lord'. To the contrary, 'if your enemy is hungry, feed him; if he is thirsty, give him something to drink; for by so doing you will heap burning coals on his head'. Do not be overcome by evil, but overcome evil with good.

In explaining that we should do good works discretely (6:1-4), Jesus wanted us to value God's reward over people's approval. This is especially important when engaged in a 'Christian' activity: if we spend time bringing what we do to the attention of others, perhaps because we want funding, then perhaps the best we can hope for in return is their money – but at the expense of God's favour.[8]

Work Parameters

When, in Matthew 6, Christ pointed to how magnificently God provides for birds and flowers, and how much more valuable people are to God, he was not implying that we could be just as passive as they could. Rather, the ways God feeds and clothes his creatures that cannot work should give confidence to those who can.

When the Promised Land was apportioned among the twelve tribes of Israel, so the settlers could provide for themselves, the law included requirements that formed the backdrop to Christ's teaching about work and which remain valid for understanding the nature and function of work today.

- God gave the land for an inheritance: it was not for exploitation in the short or medium term by whoever owned it at the time but it had to be preserved for future generations. Production had to be sustainable.

- The landowners were totally dependent on God to send rainfall in Autumn and Spring in order to get a harvest.

- The people had a duty to care for their neighbours' property and welfare. This was demonstrated by the laws of restitution about straying cattle, the damage they might do and the harm they might come to.

- The produce of the land was not for the exclusive benefit of the owners but available for the whole community. Fields could not be harvested to the edges or harvested twice, so that poor people could help themselves and not be chased away as scavengers.

---

[8] The central tragedy of modern 'Christian' fundraising is two-fold: that Christians feel the need to use the sorts of physiological tactics developed by commercial businesses and secular charities to provoke a certain percentage response from people, rather than to trust God unequivocally; that these tactics succeed in persuading Christians to give what could have been given out of simple devotion to God and love of people.

We should be just as responsible today, just as reliant on God, just as concerned about those who come after us, just as mindful of neighbours and 'rivals' and just as willing to use what we earn to help others. This fulfils Christ's fundamental command to love our neighbours as ourselves but contrary to many widely accepted norms of capitalism. We should therefore consider the following issues.

- Should we earn money in ways that do not make a positive contribution to society; activities that cause harm or perpetuate injustice?

- Should we take part in business activity that relies on exaggerating goods or services, like so much marketing, advertising and sales talk do?

- Should we do anything to exploit other people's misfortune, like increasing prices in times of shortage or need?

- Should we manipulate data (accounts, statistics and projections) for commercial or political expediency?

- Should we embellish actual performance or attainable potential in order to get customers, clients or credit?

- Should we use psychological tactics to create emotional pressure to persuade people to spend or borrow?

- Should we claim to be following up reports or surveys when we call people to sell goods and services?

- Should we try to create an illusion of authority we do not have?

- Should we rely on misdirection and convenient irrelevancies to evade responsibility for errors and poor service?

- Should we do anything suspect or sneaky to make it more difficult for a business rival to do well?

- Should we allow a colleague to fail, much less set them up for a fall, in order to gain a career advantage?

- When arguing for a promotion or pay increase, should we start by asking for more than we want, and so begin to haggle, rather than asking for what we want straightforwardly and sincerely?

- When looking for work, should we exaggerate our ability and experience on CVs and job applications?

Traditionally, Christians have been exhorted by their leaders to be exemplary employees, following the directions to slaves and servants in Ephesians 6, Colossians 3-4 and 1 Peter 2. A good example is the twelfth part of *Practical Christianity* by A W Pink, where he explains that Christian employees should be marked by honesty and integrity, fidelity and loyalty; by punctuality, truthfulness, conscientiousness, quality of work and devotion to employers' interests; by a marked absence of slackness, carelessness, selfishness, greed and insolence. This is sound advice. But although employees are not implicated in everything their employers do, and although they should not constantly be second-guessing and challenging their employers' policies and procedures, there is a line which to cross will take them into knowing collusion with unambiguous sin. Quite where that line is in any particular situation may not be obvious or easy to find but Christians should not take it for granted that shades of deception is simply the way we now live.

Spending Parameters

In our consumer society, choice is equated with liberty but then used to exploit egotism, conceit, vanity, pretention, greed, lust and other sins. We therefore ought to examine both the motives behind our spending and the benefits of what we buy. First, our motives.

- Do we, perhaps unconsciously, evaluate people by their home, possessions or income?

- Do we instinctively compare what we own to what others have?

- Are we anxious for our children to have the same status symbols and lifestyle accessories as their friends?

- Do we feel we have little choice but spend money to maintain a lifestyle that our neighbours or work colleagues expect of us?

- Are we intuitively influenced by the lifestyles portrayed in the media – on television and in newspapers and magazines?

- Does advertising create in us a desire for possessions and experiences (leisure activities and holidays) that feels almost irresistible?

- Do sales staff easily talk us into upgrading to more expensive alternatives or buying accessories we had not previously thought we wanted?

- Do we buy things sold on the back of generating fear? The latest gadgets that are less likely to break down or the latest security systems for our homes, cars and computers? Or excessive insurance and investments to insulate us against unlikely catastrophe?

- Do we buy goods and services in an effort to become better people or better liked? Things we hope will make us be, *or appear to be*, more capable, reliable, relaxed or happy?

- Are we addicted to things and experiences, like alcohol, fast food, chocolate, tobacco, shopping, exercise, gambling, music, movies and computer games?

Spending Analysis

The decisions that we make about how we use money are deeply interconnected with many other issues, such as how we feel about ourselves, who we fear and who we wish to please. As it is often easier to examine what we do than what we think, we should also examine how we use money day by day.

This scrutiny is impossible without tracking every penny we spend but, when I began teaching personal finance, I quickly realised how very difficult it is to persuade people to do it. Although it is a bother to keep a record, it seems that the greater problem is that we are afraid of what we might discover about ourselves. It is, however, worth the effort and any emotional discomfort.

It is important to record everything we buy or pay for. Every direct debit and standing order; every card and cash purchase. Every fuel bill, insurance premium, supermarket trip, DVD, bus ride, magazine, snack and sweet. Every penny spent on petrol, oil, road tax and insurance; every visit to the car wash. Every penny dropped in a church collection or charity box. Record daily purchases in a small notebook because it is very easy to forget them by the end of a day.

After a week, start to study what your daily spending has bought. It may surprise you. It will show your priorities, weaknesses and addictions; it will help you see whether you really are the person you think you are. Over a longer period, work in other expenditure to see what proportion of your total spending goes on leisure, entertainment and giving.

Ask yourself how your spending helps your spiritual growth as a Christian. Paul explained to the Corinthian church that although all things may be 'lawful' for them, they should be avoided if they work to their detriment. By 'lawful', he meant permissible: it is possible that some of them supposed that as they were not subject to the Torah, the Old Testament 'Law', but saved by God's grace, such things could never separate them from the love of Christ or annul their salvation. But Paul was concerned about what hinders fellowship with Christ, stunts spiritual growth and spoils Christian witness and gave them helpful criteria for evaluating behaviour. Putting together his comments in I Corinthians 6:12 & 10:23, we have:

All things are lawful for me, but not all things are helpful. All things are lawful for me, but I will not be enslaved by anything... All things are lawful, but not all things build up.

With this in mind, ask yourself these three questions.

Is what I buy helpful? Older translations of 6:12 read 'not expedient' and in many ways that was better because it suggested things that do not actively move us forward. Unfortunately, the word 'expedient' can now refer to things that are useful but not necessarily right: today, it is often expedient to lie or to withhold payment of an outstanding debt that could be paid without difficulty. Other modern translations say 'not beneficial' or 'not profitable'. We should reject anything that does not propel us forward to Christian maturity.

Am I enslaved by what I buy? Are they addictive – things like some drinks, sweets, entertainments, amusements and exercise? It is not only that we will keep on spending money on them but, more importantly, that they can change us. We may think that some entertainment and leisure activities seem harmless but they have the potential to stain our imagination with desires and standards of behaviour that are irreconcilable with Christ's teaching. Do we, for example, enjoy novels or movies that include gratuitous violence or strong language or that applaud vanity, greed or sexual betrayal? Do we like games that have us role-play the sort of aggression and violence we would never wish to commit in real life? Do we exercise by simulating violence? Do we enjoy music that arouses carnal feelings; do we get pleasure from dance moves that mimic sexual or sensual behaviour?

Is my spending constructive? That is, does it build up relationships and lead people to see the truth about Christ? In 1 Corinthians 10, Paul goes on to describe principles of Christian behaviour when shopping and accepting hospitality but sums up by saying that we should do *everything* to the glory of God, not seeking our own advantage but the advantage of others, 'that they may be saved'.

Avarice in the Church

This sort of self-analysis is important because money has snared Christians from the start and we should not think that we are immune. Ananias and his wife Sapphira sold land and gave the proceeds to the Jerusalem church.[9] Unfortunately, they kept back some of the money but said they had donated everything. Why did they heed the satanic impulse and conspire together to lie? Did they wish to appear more generous than they actually were, in order to improve their social standing in the church? Or did they keep some of the money as security, 'for a rainy day', but not want to appear to have weak or compromised faith in God? Whatever their motive, money was more important to them than it ought to have been and it led them into sin!

James' epistle is not addressed to just one church but to many and it was probably the first of the New Testament epistles to be written. The problems mentioned include preferential treatment for rich people, despising the poor, hoarding wealth, laying business plans without reference to God and cheating employees out of their wages.

At Corinth, Christian business people cheated each other and then dragged each other through the courts. As Christ said that it would be by their love for one another that people would recognise his disciples, these Christians must have severely damaged the church's witness! 'Why not rather suffer wrong?' Paul wrote, 'Why not rather be defrauded?'[10]

It is sobering to think that Paul probably did not expect his warning to Timothy about avarice to be heeded. In his next letter to Timothy, he wrote, 'But understand this, that in the last days there will come times of difficulty. For people will be lovers of self, lovers of money, proud, arrogant, abusive… heartless, unappeasable, slanderous, without self-control, brutal, not loving good, treacherous, reckless, swollen with

---

[9] For a complete picture of what happened read Acts 4:32-5:11.
[10] 1 Corinthians 6:1-10.

conceit, lovers of pleasure rather than lovers of God.' He then makes it clear that he is referring to Christians or, at least, to people who attend church: 'having *the appearance of godliness*, but denying its power'.[11] The pursuit of wealth is always incompatible with Christian progress.

In the 4th Century, John Cassian warned against corrupting Christ's words, 'It is more blessed to give than to receive', to justify avarice and greed – rationalising that if they get more, they can then give more! In the 19th Century, Charles Finney warned Christians about the dangers of 'conforming to the world' in business practice in order to make money that could be used to fund good works and help to expand the Kingdom of God. He said, 'A holy church, that would act on the principles of the gospel, would spread the gospel faster that all the money that ever was in New York, or ever will be'.

I have met Christians in business who believe that if something is not illegal it cannot be sinful. Some are so acclimatised to their environment, they behave no differently to the most unscrupulous of their colleagues. It is still worse when they are engaged in charitable or church work.[12] It seems that a subjective certainty in the rightness of their 'calling' trumps any objective code of conduct derived from the scriptures: if, therefore, deception, deceit or dishonesty is necessary to achieve their goal, they cannot see it as sinful.

Still more worrying are the more commonplace ways in which Christians conform to the norms of modern society. Christians who would not lie on their CVs nevertheless boast of their abilities and achievements with little objectivity and contrary to the Christian virtues of modesty and humility.[13] I have been asked to help Christians with money problems, only to discover they were fiddling their tax return or Benefit claim

---

[11] 2 Timothy 3:1-5. Paul adds, 'Avoid such people'.

[12] We ought to be careful to distinguish between 'Christian' charities run by Christians to Biblical standards and charities that promote themselves as 'Christian' because they see Christians and churches as their niche market.

[13] See, for example, Proverbs 27:2, Romans 12:3, Philippians 2:3 & 1 Peter 5:5.

or had obtained credit by bending the truth. While there may have been no material link between their dishonesty and their financial problems, I suspect there was a spiritual one: 'The Lord disciplines the one he loves, and chastises every son whom he receives'.[14]

The Misunderstood Manager

Christ's parables portray the sort of lifestyle he described in the Sermon on the Mount, although having grown up with capitalism we can easily misread them. The parable of the dishonest manager (or unjust steward) is probably the most misunderstood.[15]

There are three common mistakes:

- The manager was dishonest because he wasted his master's goods.
- Reducing the debts owed to his master was dishonest.
- Christ commended the manager's shrewdness.

The manager may have been underhand in wasting his master's goods but he is not accused of theft, fraud or any 'serious' dishonesty: if he had been, his master would not have told him to make up the accounts but put him in prison until everything was repaid! The accusation can also be translated as 'squandering' and so I expect he was doing the sorts of things many workers do: exaggerating time spent at work, slacking and pilfering. There is a long history to this sort of behaviour in the UK: 'Every Englishman has his fiddle' is folklore so old and well established that it is practically part of the Common Law! The manager's behaviour was, however, an indication of what was to follow.

The manager was not dishonest for reducing the debts owed to his master because it was within his delegated authority to do it. Moreover, it was the morally right thing to do. The debtors were probably the master's tenants who

---

[14] Hebrews 12:6.
[15] Luke 16:1-15.

owed rent, although they may have been customers who owed payment for goods. The manager was responsible for the master's business and, consequently, he was responsible for the welfare of not just the tenants and others who did business with his master but also their families. Making the reductions was therefore the responsible social action: the rich creditor who did not need the money reduced the amounts owed by poor people who did.

The manager was dishonest because he did this *for his own ends*. He moved beyond wasting his master's goods to bartering them for his personal advantage, to secure his own future. If a bank executive today wrote off a debt on compassionate grounds, we would think it a good use of the executive's discretion; if, however, we learn that the executive expected a personal benefit in return, we would question his integrity.

The dishonest manager was commended by his master for his shrewdness and this raises an interesting point. Did the master think the manager was shrewd because he finally did the right thing, simply because it was the right thing to do? Or did he know about the manager's fraudulent self-interest and realise that he could turn that cunning to his own advantage? I do not know but, crucially, Christ did *not* commend the manager's shrewdness.

Christ did, however, note that, 'The sons of this world are more shrewd in dealing with their own generation than the sons of light'. In other words, ordinary men and women living according to the ways of society will do what is right when it is in their own self-interest but the children of light, Christians, are not usually so pragmatic about Kingdom standards and lifestyle. Nevertheless, we should not conclude from this that Christ wants us to be just as selfishly pragmatic as the dishonest manager!

On another occasion, Christ told a parable about an unjust judge to encourage his disciples to persevere in prayer.[16] The

---

[16] Luke 18:1-8.

judge did not fear God or respect people but he gave justice to an aggrieved widow when her persistent badgering began to annoy him. Was Christ saying that God is like that judge? Or did Christ expect us to realise how just and loving God is in comparison to the unjust judge?

Similarly, Christ does not want us to be like the selfish, dishonest manager. He does not, for example, want us to be good to our business rivals and work colleagues *only* because we expect something later. What he really wants is for us to do the right thing, and to do it cheerfully, because it is the right thing to do. Even where money is involved.

Deliberate Choices

Christ's other parables also show ways to handle money contrary to the norms of capitalism. In the parable of the vineyard workers, the owner hires people at 6am, 9am, noon and 3pm but at the end of the day pays them all the same wage.[17] There is a clear spiritual application but, equally, a practical one. The owner had promised to pay each worker 'whatever is right' and so paid them all the daily living wage. Most of them, and many people today, cannot see how this can be right, but the owner was ensuring the welfare of *all* the workers and their families, for the good of society as a whole.

By contrast, the rich farmer was foolish when he decided to hoard his abundant harvest.[18] He had been dependent on God for it and, contrary to what many suppose, did not have an exclusive right to it. He should have thought about the needs of his workers, their families and the community as well his own future. In the story of the rich man and Lazarus, the rich man was condemned because he ignored poor, sick Lazarus: he did not mistreat or abuse Lazarus, he just ignored the man in need sitting by his gate.[19]

---

[17] Matthew 20:1-16.

[18] Luke 12:16-21.

[19] Luke 16:19-31. The rich man who ignored Lazarus seemed to have had little regard even for the welfare of his own servants, the people living *within* his gate, if the

This is not reading too much into the parables. They were stories of daily life meant to help people understand spiritual truths and therefore had to mirror Christ's own understanding of how life should be lived.

In Acts 2, we read how the first Christians lived. As well as being devoted to teaching and the sacraments, and seeing signs and wonders, and leading people to faith in Christ, they 'had all things in common [and] were selling their possessions and belongings and distributing the proceeds to all, as any had need'. They were not living in a commune and were by no means communists (they retained private ownership) but their possessions no longer held the same importance: people, especially God's people, were far more important to them.

The Desert Fathers were Christians who responded to the 'Christianisation' of the Roman Empire by retreating into the hard isolation of the desert. While I cannot endorse everything they did and said, their discipleship was not compromised by financial concerns. 'When buying or selling you can hardly avoid sin', one of them wrote. 'So, in either case, be sure you lose a little in the transaction. Do not haggle about the price for love of gain, and so indulge in actions harmful to the soul – quarrelling, lying, shifting your ground and so on – thus bringing our way of life into disrepute.'

The hermits made things they could sell at market, in order to get the money they needed to buy food and other supplies. One of them is remembered because he sold what he made to the people who most needed it for whatever price they could afford and then bought what he needed from the traders who most needed his custom, for whatever price they asked.

The degree to which we, today, can live like this will depend on the extent to which we trust God to underwrite our obedience to Christ's teaching.

---

observation that he 'feasted sumptuously every day' is meant to imply they were not allowed a day off on the Sabbath.